In the Footsteps of Explorers

Ferdinand Magellan

Circumnavigating the World

Katharine Bailey

Crabtree Publishing Company

www.crabtreebooks.com

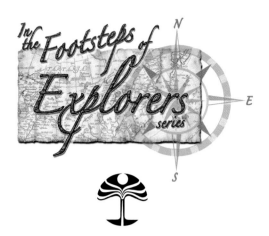

Crabtree Publishing Company

www.crabtreebooks.com

For my Mum and Dad

Coordinating editor: Ellen Rodger
Series editor: Carrie Gleason
Editors: Rachel Eagen, Adrianna Morganelli
Design and production coordinator: Rosie Gowsell
Cover design and production assistance: Samara Parent
Art direction: Rob MacGregor
Scanning technician: Arlene Arch-Wilson
Photo research: Allison Napier

Consultants: Stacy Hasselbacher and Tracey Neikirk, The Mariners' Museum, Newport News, Virginia

Photo Credits: The Art Archive/ Marine Museum Lisbon/ Dagli Orti: cover; Giraudon/ Art Resource, NY: p. 9, p. 29 (bottom); Erich Lessing/ Art Resource, NY: p. 8; Scala/ Art Resource, NY: p. 6 (bottom); Private Collection/ Bridgeman Art Library: p. 15; Bettmann/ Corbis: p. 18; Dean Conger/ Corbis: p. 26; Jack Fields/ Corbis: p. 21, p. 24, p. 27; Lindsay Hebberd/ Corbis: p. 20; Chris Hellier/ Corbis: p. 7; Wolfgang Kaehler/ Corbis: p. 30; Charles O'Rear/ Corbis: p. 22; Royalty Free/ Corbis: p. 17; STScI/ NASA/ Ressmeyer/ Corbis: p. 31; Lawson Wood/ Corbis: p. 14;

The Granger Collection, New York: p. 13; istock Photo: p. 12, p. 16; North Wind / North Wind Picture Archives: p. 5, p. 11, p. 19, p. 23, p. 25 (bottom); Other images from stock photo cd

Illustrations: Adrianna Morganelli: p. 4; Lauren Fast: p. 7

Cartography: Jim Chernishenko: title page, p. 10

Cover: Ferdinand Magellan was a Portuguese navigator and sea captain who commanded a fleet for Spain that was the first to circumnavigate, or sail around, the world. Magellan did not survive the voyage and was killed in the Philippines.

Title page: The Armada de Molucca, a group of five ships commanded by Magellan, left Spain in 1519. The fleet sailed around the world: west to the New World, and then on to Indonesia and back home. Only one of five ships and a handful of men returned to Spain after three years at sea.

Sidebar icon: A wooden sailing ship of the Age of Exploration.

Crabtree Publishing Company

www.crabtreebooks.com   1-800-387-7650

Cataloging-in-Publication Data

Bailey, Katharine, 1980-
   Ferdinand Magellan : circumnavigating the world / written by Katharine Bailey.
      p. cm. -- (In the footsteps of explorers)
   Includes index.
   ISBN-13: 978-0-7787-2416-2 (rlb)
   ISBN-10: 0-7787-2416-6 (rlb)
   ISBN-13: 978-0-7787-2452-0 (pb)
   ISBN-10: 0-7787-2452-2 (pb)
   1. Magellan, Ferdinand, 1521--Juvenile literature. 2. Explorers--Portugal--Biography--Juvenile literature. 3. Voyages around the world--Juvenile literature. I. Title. II. Series.
   G286.M2B22 2005
   910'.92--dc22   2005014943
                                                              LC

Published in the United States
PMB 16A
350 Fifth Ave.
Suite 3308
New York, NY
10118

Published in Canada
616 Welland Ave.
St. Catharines
Ontario, Canada
L2M 5V6

Published in the United Kingdom
73 Lime Walk
Headington
Oxford
OX3 7AD
United Kingdom

Published in Australia
386 Mt. Alexander Rd.
Ascot Vale (Melbourne)
VIC 3032

Contents

The Lure of Spice

Ferdinand Magellan captained the first fleet of ships to circumnavigate, or sail around, the world. His mission was to discover a westward passage from Spain to the Spice Islands, an almost mythical chain of islands in the Far East also called the Moluccas.

(above) Magellan did not live to see the Spice Islands. Of the five ships and hundreds of men who left Spain in 1519, only one ship returned.

A Fortune to be Found

The goal of Magellan's voyage was to discover a westward sea passage from Spain to the Moluccas, a collection of tiny islands between the Pacific Ocean and the Indian Ocean. Magellan's fleet was looking for valuable spices, such as nutmeg and cloves, which grew on the islands. Spices were treasured and expensive, and were used as medicines and to help food taste better. During the 1500s, the European countries of Portugal and Spain raced to claim the islands as their own. The country that controlled the Spice Islands would be very rich and powerful.

A Sailor's Quest

Magellan was born in Portugal and served in its royal **court**. He trained as a **navigator** and sailed with Portuguese fleets to countries such as Africa and India. Like many explorers, he dreamed of finding a sea route to the Spice Islands. He asked the Portuguese king to approve a voyage to the islands. It was denied and Magellan went to Spain to seek permission. The Spanish king agreed to **finance** the voyage and gave him a fleet of five ships.

Finding the Strait

Magellan's plan to sail westward around the world to the Spice Islands depended on finding a **strait** through the continent of South America. This journal entry by fleet diarist Antonio Pigafetta from October 1520, describes sighting the strait. Magellan was known as the Captain General because he commanded the entire fleet.

"Had it not been for the Captain General, we would not have found that strait, for we all thought and said that it was closed on all sides. But the Captain General, who knew where to sail and sent two ships to discover what was inside the cape of the bay. The ships, the San Antonio and the Concepción were sent to discover what was inside the cape of the bay. Approaching the end of the bay, and thinking that they were lost, they saw a small opening which did not appear to be an opening, but a sharp turn. Like desperate men they hauled into it, and thus they discovered the strait by chance . . .

(below) The passage around the southern tip of South America from the Atlantic Ocean to the Pacific Ocean is now called the Strait of Magellan.

– 1480 –
Magellan born
Fernão de
Magalhães in
Sabrosa,
Portugal.

– 1517 –
**Magellan moves
to Spain and
declares loyalty
to the
Spanish king.**

– 1519 –
**Armada de
Molucca sails
from Seville .**

– 1521 –
**Magellan is
killed in battle
in the
Philippines.**

A World Divided

In the 1400s, Europe entered the Age of Discovery, a new era of European world exploration. Portugal and Spain led the way into this new age by sending explorers on missions to discover new trading routes and claim new lands for their countries.

A World Divided

Portugal dominated much of the known trading routes during this time. The Treaty of Tordesillas, an agreement between Spain and Portugal, divided the world in half between the two countries. An imaginary line was drawn down the middle of the Atlantic Ocean, with Portugal given the lands east of the line and Spain given the lands west.

(left) King Charles I of Spain wanted the wealth that control of the spice trade would bring.

King Charles' Spain

King Charles I of Spain was a young and ambitious ruler. He ruled Spain, but wanted to be emperor of the **Holy Roman Empire** as well. He spent a lot of money pursuing this title, leaving him with little to govern Spain. To **replenish** Spain's wealth, King Charles wanted to open trade routes to the East and its valuable spices.

The Casa de Contratación

The Casa de Contratación, or the House of Commerce, controlled all of the expeditions that sailed for Spain. This government agency outfitted ships, imposed punishments on crews, and had control of the sea charts needed for navigating. King Charles needed the Casa's leader, Bishop Fonseca, to approve Magellan's voyage. Fonseca asked the Spanish banking house, the House of Fugger, for most of the funds.

The Spanish Inquisition

In the late 1400s and 1500s, most people in Spain practiced a denomination, or division, of **Christianity** called **Roman Catholicism**. Spain's rulers wanted everyone to be Catholic. In 1478, a court called the Spanish Inquisition was set up to investigate whether or not people were practicing Catholicism. Punishment for not following the religion was torture and death. Thousands of people died as a result of the Inquisition. Many people **converted** to Catholicism from other religions in order to escape punishment. The beliefs of the Inquisition even spread to the ships of discovery that sailed from Spanish ports. Priests were sent along as part of the crews and conducted **mass** and prayers every day. Magellan held the power of life and death over his crew and used Inquisition torture methods to punish those who committed crimes, or offenses.

(right) Victims of the Inquisition were tortured using devices such as the strappado. Magellan used similar methods to punish crew members for offenses.

– 1492 –

Sailing for Spain, Christopher Columbus (above) reaches the New World.

– 1498 –

Vasco de Gama sails to India from Spain, establishing an important trade route for Portugal.

– 1515 –

Spaniard Juan de Solis tries to find the strait.

Young Magellan

Magellan spent his youth as a page in Portugal's royal court. There, he learned many skills such as how to read the stars, how to wield a sword, and how to ride a horse.

Sailing for Portugal

When he was 25 years old, Magellan joined a Portuguese fleet of ships captained by Francisco de Almeida. They sailed to India and fought to establish a Portuguese trading post.

Successes and Troubles

Magellan had many successes at sea. He was promoted up the ranks of crew and had a goal to command his own fleet. These dreams were almost dashed when he was accused of stealing during a battle in Morocco, in North Africa. He was proven innocent of the crime, but Portugal's King Manuel remained angry with him. He refused to allow Magellan to lead a voyage of exploration.

Refused Again

Magellan asked King Manuel three times if he would sponsor a voyage to the Spice Islands. Each time he was turned down. After his final refusal, he asked the king if he could look to another country for support and was granted permission.

Siding with Spain

In Portugal, Magellan met Ruy Faleiro, a cosmologist who studied the Earth's place among the stars and planets. Faleiro and Magellan decided that the Spice Islands were likely located in territory considered Spanish according to the Treaty of Tordesillas. They believed they could reach the islands by sailing west through an undiscovered strait that cut through South America. Magellan proposed this idea to King Charles I of Spain. A westward route would avoid Portuguese waters and give Spain access to the riches of the Far East. King Charles agreed to the proposal and gave Magellan a **commission** to sail to the Spice Islands.

(left) Navigators used astrolabes to determine their ships' locations. In Portugal, Magellan trained to use instruments of navigation.

The Armada de Molucca

King Charles got approval from the Casa de Contratación, who organized funding, bought the ships, and hired over 200 crew members. Magellan ensured the ships were in good repair and arranged to buy enough provisions for two years at sea. The ships were filled with trading goods, barrels of wine, salted fish and meat, preserved fruit, and hardtack, the sailor's bread. The fleet was called the Armada de Molucca.

(background) Seville was a bustling Spanish port and center of trade. Located on the Quadalquivir River, it was the Armada de Molucca's home port.

The Armada Sets Sail

From the beginning, the voyage of the Armada de Molucca involved many people with competing interests. Magellan's Portuguese nationality caused many problems. The Spanish public was outraged that a Portuguese commanded their ships, and the Armada's crew distrusted their leader.

Early Signs of Trouble

The Casa de Contratación selected most of Magellan's officers and crew. Spanish officers were awarded the best positions on the ships. The Spanish sailors thought Magellan was a Portuguese spy leading them into a trap. Magellan made things worse by giving family members important positions on the ships.

A Letter Arrives

The Armada, which consisted of five ships, left Seville in August 1519. The fleet stopped in the Canary Islands where Magellan received a letter from his father-in-law. The letter revealed a crew plot to **mutiny** and seize command of the ships. The would-be mutineer was Juan de Cartagena, captain of one of the Armada's ships. He believed Magellan had stolen the position of Captain General and wanted to take command.

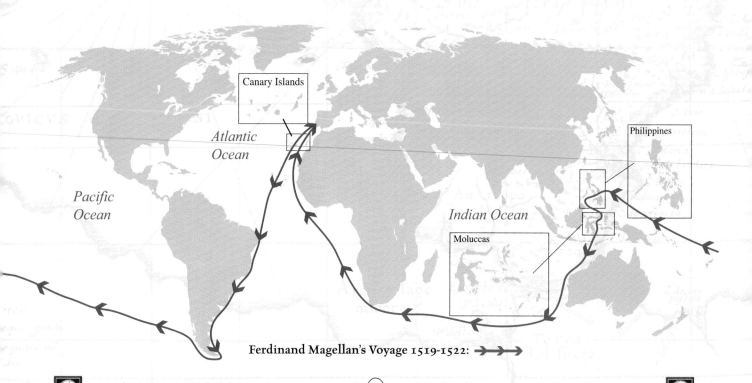

Canary Islands

Atlantic Ocean

Pacific Ocean

Indian Ocean

Philippines

Moluccas

Ferdinand Magellan's Voyage 1519-1522: ➤➤➤

Across the Atlantic

The Armada sailed down the coast of Africa and soon the rumors contained in the letter were confirmed. Cartagena tried to start a mutiny by challenging Magellan's orders and refusing to obey them. Magellan responded by arresting Cartagena and locking him in **stocks** on the deck. The Armada sailed across the Atlantic to South America. It stopped in Rio de Janeiro, Brazil, for two weeks before continuing south down the coast to search for the strait that would lead to the Pacific. The fleet endured two months of severe storms before Magellan called a halt to the search. He ordered the Armada's crew to set up a camp on land for the winter.

Discontent

Magellan built the camp Port St. Julian. He cut the crew's daily **rations** to save food for the long winter ahead. This angered the crew, who had expected to be rewarded for their hard work during the storms. They also began to question Magellan's ability to lead them to the strait, if it even existed. Their fear of death at sea was stronger than their faith in their Captain General.

(above) The ships of the Armada de Molucca, the Trinidad, Concepción, San Antonio, Victoria, and Santiago, endured rough seas and weather. Magellan sailed aboard the Trinidad.

Mutiny and Mayhem

After months at sea enduring storms and their captain's relentless search for a passage to the Pacific, Magellan's crew was angry. Cartagena took advantage of their anger to plot another mutiny. This time, the result was murder.

Mutiny

Relieved of duty after his previous attempt to mutiny, Cartagena tried again. The captains of the *San Antonio*, *Concepción*, and *Victoria* joined him and tried to take control of the fleet. Magellan was one step ahead of their plans and even intercepted messages sent from the *Concepción* to the other ships involved in the mutiny. Magellan recaptured the *Victoria* by having one of his men slash its captain Luis de Mendoza's throat. He also recaptured the *San Antonio*. After seeing that Magellan had recaptured the two ships, the *Concepción* surrendered.

(above) Magellan struck back at his mutineers and had one disloyal captain's throat slit with a knife. The captain's body was later drawn and quartered and his head was put on a pole and displayed as an example to others.

Crime and Punishment

Magellan punished the leaders of the mutiny with torture or death. Forty men sentenced to death had their sentences **commuted** to hard labor. Some mutineers were tortured using the methods of the Inquisition. Cartagena and a mutinous priest were marooned, or left behind, at Port St. Julian when the ships left. Magellan's harsh punishment of the mutineers made the rest of his crew fear and loathe him.

Shipwreck

A month after the mutiny, Magellan sent the *Santiago*, the Armada's smallest ship, down the coast to look for the strait. It shipwrecked many miles away and sank. Two survivors risked their lives to bring news of the shipwreck back to Magellan, who sent a rescue party. Now with only four ships, Magellan ordered the fleet to wait out the winter in Port St. Julian. They waited five months to resume the search for the strait.

The *San Antonio* Mutiny

In mid-October, the *Trinidad's* **pilot** spotted the opening to the long searched for strait. Magellan sent the *Concepción* and *San Antonio* ahead to look for possible routes through the strait. Once the *San Antonio* was out of sight, a mutiny broke out onboard. The *San Antonio's* pilot took over from its captain, who was Magellan's cousin. He set a course back to Spain with most of the Armada's food and water stored onboard.

Sailing the Strait

Magellan and the remaining three ships continued on through the strait. For 38 days, the Armada passed lands of fire, giant glaciers, and dense forests. Finally, they reached the end of the strait and found a **cape** that opened up into the Pacific Ocean. Magellan did not know he faced the largest body of water in the world. Their maps incorrectly showed a small stretch of water between South America and Asia. Magellan wrongly expected that the Armada's destination, the Spice Islands, was merely a few days of sailing away.

(background) The Armada spent agonizing months searching for the strait that would lead from the Atlantic to the Pacific oceans.

Life at Sea

The Armada de Molucca's five ships were made for shipping cargo in and out of Spain's shallow-water port of Seville. They each took specialized workers thousands of hours to build and required constant maintenance at sea. During Magellan's voyage, over 200 men of many nationalities labored day and night to keep the ships in working order.

The Ships

Each ship in the Armada had a name: the *Trinidad, Concepción, San Antonio, Victoria,* and *Santiago.* The fleet's largest ship was the *San Antonio.* It carried most of the fleet's provisions. The measurement of how much cargo a ship could carry was called a *tonelada,* or Spanish ton. A *tonelada* was the space occupied by two barrels, or casks, of wine. The *San Antonio* carried 120 *tonelada* and the smallest, the *Santiago,* carried 75 *tonelada.* The ships were very tall and most of their hulls, or bodies, and **masts** were painted black with tar. Tar sealed the seams in the hull so that water did not seep through. Each ship had three square or triangular sails and multiple decks.

(right) Flying fish sometimes flopped on the ships' decks while at sea.

Rank and Privilege

The crew was divided by rank. Pages, or ship's boys, were the lowest rank and were usually young boys. They scrubbed the decks, cleaned up after meals, and did chores. Sailors and their **apprentices** made up the next rank. Above that were the specialists. Gunners were considered specialists because operating weaponry was a dangerous job. Trained pilots and navigators steered the ships, read the charts and weather, and kept the fleet on course.

(below) The seams of the ship were caulked with tar on a regular basis, either in shallow water or on shore.

VICTORIA.

The ship's cargo contained everything the crew of the Armada de Molucca needed for their voyage. It included trading goods, weaponry, food, clothing, and supplies for cleaning and repair. The trading cargo included mirrors (above), bolts of cloth, red hats, bells, and more. These were exchanged for food and spices during the voyage.

The Ship's Cargo

The fleet's cargo included a large store of weapons. They were for defense against pirates, the Portuguese, or battles with the people they met on their way. Magellan often fired cannons or guns to scare, or impress, the native peoples when he arrived at a new place.

(below left) Magellan and several of his officers unknowingly prevented getting scurvy by regularly eating a jam made from quince, a fruit similar to an apple. It was not widely known until the late 1700s that the vitamin C absorbed by eating fruit prevented scurvy. Scurvy was a disease that loosened teeth, and weakened and eventually killed many sailors.

(below) Every crew member was given a daily ration. Food packed for the trip included honey, nuts, cheese, raisins, chickpeas, prunes, and wine for drinking.

WINE

Coconut Milk

The people of Cebu, an island in the Philippines where the Armada stopped, often drank fresh coconut juice or made coconut milk. Here's how you can make your own:

What you need:
Coconut
2 cups of water
electric food processor
strainer
oven mitts
oven preset to low heat

What to do:
1. Ask an adult to split a coconut in half.
2. Save the clear juice inside.
3. Place the two halves of the coconut in the oven at low heat to dry the skin a bit.
4. Remove the halves carefully with oven mitts.
5. With a fork, carefully peel off the brown skin.
6. Place the white pieces of coconut meat in the food processor.
7. Add the water, or the coconut's juice, and blend at high speed until completely mixed.
8. Strain out liquid and enjoy.

(right) The sailors ate coconut when they reached the Philippines.

(background) Sailors wore loose fitting pants and shirts made of rough cotton. Each man had a chest where he stored clothes and personal items, such as playing cards.

Disaster and Death

Magellan thought the journey to the Spice Islands would be short. He was wrong. It took the Armada de Molucca 98 grueling days to cross the Pacific Ocean. The ships did not contain enough food and water for the voyage and most of the crew fell ill, and died from scurvy and starvation.

The Philippines

After four months at sea, the Armada sailed into what is now called the Philippine Islands. Magellan befriended the king of the island of Limasawa and persuaded him to become a Christian. Magellan continued his conversions on the nearby island of Cebu where he and his crew were treated to feasts. The leaders of the nearby island of Mactan refused to convert and Magellan showed them how powerful he was by burning a Mactan village to the ground.

(below) Magellan scared and impressed the islanders by firing his cannons and guns. He began to feel that his weapons and men were superior to the natives of the Philippines.

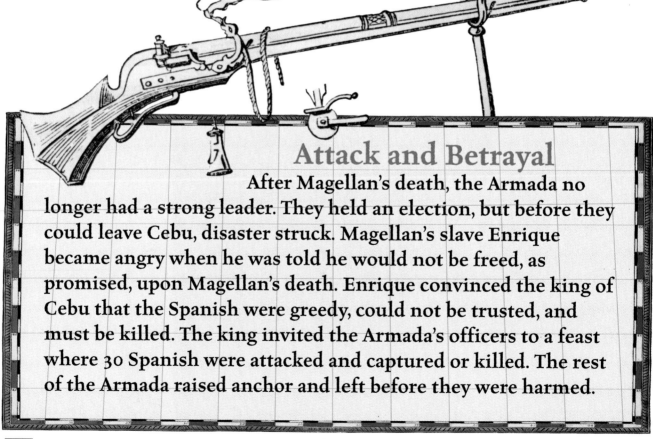

Attack and Betrayal

After Magellan's death, the Armada no longer had a strong leader. They held an election, but before they could leave Cebu, disaster struck. Magellan's slave Enrique became angry when he was told he would not be freed, as promised, upon Magellan's death. Enrique convinced the king of Cebu that the Spanish were greedy, could not be trusted, and must be killed. The king invited the Armada's officers to a feast where 30 Spanish were attacked and captured or killed. The rest of the Armada raised anchor and left before they were harmed.

Magellan Dies

Magellan's success in converting the Cebuans to Christianity made him feel very powerful. He became involved in a rivalry between the Cebuans and the peoples of the island of Mactan. Magellan arranged to fight the Mactans, believing that one of his men equaled 100 natives in battle. He thought he could easily overpower them. Instead, thousands of Mactan natives, armed with poison-tipped arrows and spears, fought just 60 of Magellan's men. Magellan was killed in the battle, along with eight of his men. His crew watched from their ships offshore, refusing to send reinforcements or even to collect Magellan's body.

(background) Magellan is killed on the island of Mactan.

The Spice Islands

Escaping from the massacre at Cebu, the surviving crew of the Armada set a course for the Spice Islands. So many navigators and experienced sailors had been lost in the massacre that the remaining crew did not know the route. They kidnapped passing sailors and native islanders who directed them to the Moluccas.

Sailing and Searching

The Armada drifted from island to island in what is today the Philippines and Indonesia. The ships also landed in Brunei and the crews rested there. The island people were used to seeing foreigners, as the Chinese and **Arabs** had long established trading ties. The Armada exchanged gifts and attended feasts with the leaders and kings of the islands. In the islands of Indonesia, the crew spent over a month repairing their ships, which had begun to rot.

(above) Cloves are the flower buds of a tree that grew only in the rich, volcanic soil of Indonesia's Spice Islands, the Moluccas. Cloves, nutmeg, and pepper were valuable spices and a ship full of spices was worth the trip.

At Last!

In November 1521, the Armada landed at the Spice Island called Tidore, a volcanic island where the beaches smelled of cloves. Tidore's leader, Almanzor, was eager to trade and soon the hulls of the *Trinidad* and *Victoria* were full of valuable cloves. The *Trinidad* was so full it sprung a leak when they tried to leave. The *Victoria* left the *Trinidad* and its crew behind for repairs and sailed for Spain under the command of Juan Sebastian Elcano, one of the 40 men who had earlier mutinied under Magellan.

End of the Trinidad

The *Trinidad* never returned to Spain. After repairs, it set sail for Spain, only to get lost and retrace its steps to Tidore. The Portuguese had arrived in Tidore during their absence. When the *Trinidad* arrived, the Portuguese captured, killed, or enslaved the crew and left the empty *Trinidad* to shipwreck off Tidore's coast.

1521

– April 27 –
Magellan dies in the Battle of Mactan.

– May 21 –
The *San Antonio* arrives back in Seville, Spain.

– May –
The *Concepción* is burned, and the fleet resumes the voyage.

– November –
The Armada sight the Spice Islands.

(above) The Moluccas, or Spice Islands, as they were called, are a group of thousands of islands in present-day Indonesia. In the 1500s, only five islands were considered to be part of the Moluccas. Their names are: Ternate, Tidore, Motir, Makian, and Bacan.

The Journey Home

The last ship of the fleet endured a long, hard journey across the Indian Ocean, trying to avoid Portuguese territory for fear of being caught. They reached home with just 18 men, but their precious cargo, the reason for their journey, remained intact.

(background) The Cape of Good Hope, the southern end of South Africa, was known as the Cape of Storms to early sailors.

Cape of Fears

The *Victoria*'s crew was hungry and dying of scurvy by the time they reached the famed Cape of Good Hope at the tip of Africa. The cape, known for its extremely rough waters and high winds, was feared by sailors. Many ships sunk attempting to round the cape from the Indian Ocean to the Atlantic Ocean. The *Victoria*'s crew made many attempts to sail it. The ship leaked and the winds, storms, and **riptides** threatened to tear it apart. Luckily, a lull in the weather allowed the *Victoria* to safely round the cape and head north to Spain.

The Fate of the *San Antonio*

The *San Antonio* sailed from the Armada at the Strait of Magellan. The crew could no longer take Magellan's brutal authority and sailed back to Spain, arriving in Spring 1521. The ship did not stop to search for or rescue Cartagena or the priest who Magellan had abandoned for mutiny. In Spain, some of the *San Antonio's* crew were thrown in jail, but most escaped without punishment.

Home to Seville

When the *Victoria* returned to the port of Seville, Spain, it was a horrible sight. Only 18 men out of the original 200 survived the three-year journey. The remaining men were sick and as thin as skeletons, but their role in history was made: they were the first to circumnavigate the world.

Shipload of Money

The king was glad to have the ship full of spices return. The *Victoria's* hull contained enough cloves to earn a profit for the voyage. The king held several trials in court to determine what happened during the voyage. There were many different sides of the story. Some crew members told the courts that Magellan was a brave leader who cared for his men. Others told stories of Magellan as a killer and careless leader. In time, some of the crew members received official **commendations** from the king for their success.

(above) The Victoria was the only ship of the Armada to survive. The San Antonio, piloted by mutineers, returned to Spain from South America the year before, after escaping at the Strait of Magellan.

Friendship and Fear

The Armada de Molucca met many indigenous, or native peoples, during their journey. Their encounters were often recorded in crew members' journals. Indigenous peoples saved their lives by offering them food and shelter while receiving little in return.

South American Giants

The Teheulche Indians, who Magellan called the Pathagoni, or Big Feet people, lived near Port St. Julian, the Armada's camp in South America. One of the Armada's diarists, an Italian named Antonio Pigafetta, attempted to learn their language. He described the Teheulche's clothing and large boots made of animal skins and their faces painted in red and yellow. The Armada kidnapped one Pathagonian, but the man died on the journey through the Pacific.

(below) The Cebuans, or Cebuano, performed at feasts held for the ships of the Armada. Here, a cultural group recreates the historic events.

Houses on Stilts

The homes of Cebu were arranged along the water's edge. They were built on stilts in groups of five or six. Networks of fishing lines were constructed near the shoreside homes and the islanders fished and farmed for food. Palm trees were used for making wine, and cloth for their clothing. They also ate coconut meat and drank its juice. Fruits such as bananas, which the Spaniards thought were figs, and nuts also grew on the island.

INSVLA MATHAN

Victoria

Doing Business

When the Armada reached the Philippines and later, the Spice Islands, they began trading goods such as silver and cloth with each island's *rajah*, or king. The *rajahs* controlled the trading of goods and the exchange of presents, such as food or gold. The *rajahs* of Cebu and Limasawa appeared to be wealthy. They ordered great feasts for the Europeans and wore jewelry of gold and precious gems.

(left) An early map shows Magellan's ships and men and the island of Mactan in the Philippines, where the Cebuan, or Cebuano, people lived.

Trade Mission

In Brazil, the Armada's crew purchased food with knives and fishhooks, which the native Guarani people valued for hunting. In other cases, trading went badly. On an island now called Guam, a misunderstanding about trading resulted in the death of many of the island's native peoples.

Arms and Power

Sometimes, Magellan sought to establish good trading relationships by impressing native populations with his store of weapons. He would fire deafening **mortars** off when arriving in a port, assuring the local people it was a sign of goodwill. In Cebu, Magellan amazed Rajah Kolambu, the island's king, with a demonstration of body armor. He had one of his crew strike an armored crew member with knives. The weapon's inability to pierce the armor awed the people of Cebu and made Magellan look like a very powerful leader.

Trading Partners

The most successful trading experience the Armada had was in the Spice Islands. The crew of the Armada had learned valuable lessons in their travels. They left with their precious cargo of spices and avoided confrontations with the local population. The people of the Spice Islands were used to trading with other nations. They had traded with the Chinese and the Arabs for hundreds of years. In the late 1400s and early 1500s, their main trading partners were the Portuguese.

(left) The ships' journals recorded many island people having blackened mouths from chewing betal, a mixture of betal tree leaves, lime, and areca nut, that made people feel good.

Relations with Native Peoples

As the Armada de Molucca sailed around the world, the native peoples they met provided vital supplies. Magellan and other crew members traded for fresh food and water. They were given hunting tips or information about safe places to sail their ships. Myths, rumors, and suspicion often influenced how Magellan and his crew treated these people. Stories of crude customs such as **cannibalism** made sailors fear the ships' every stop. These stories were rarely based on fact, but the crew believed them.

(background) Rusting cannons on the Spice Island of Ternate, Indonesia. Europeans guarded the island territory they took over.

After Magellan

The journey of the Armada de Molucca began a new chapter in sea travel for Europeans. It also renewed the debate about who the valuable Spice Islands belonged to. King Charles claimed them for his own, while Portugal claimed they were located in its half of the world.

Costly and Risky

The discovery of the new trade route did not mean immediate wealth for Spain. Sailing west from Spain to the Spice Islands was a dangerous journey. The ships were too small and too slow for sailing around the world and many were lost. The venture was both costly and risky.

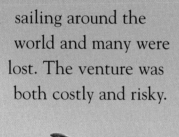

More Expeditions

King Charles dispatched three different expeditions to retrace Magellan's route to the chain of islands. All three failed, putting him deeply into debt with the House of Fugger. This enormous debt forced King Charles to borrow money from Portugal and lose his claim to the Spice Islands. In 1529, the ownership of the islands was settled. In an agreement to borrow money from King Joao III of Portugal, King Charles was forced to give the Spice Islands to Portugal under the Treaty of Saragossa.

(left) Magellan's voyage was the first to discover the power of the Pacific trade winds as they sailed west from South America. The crew also noted penguins, or "featherless black geese" on the southern tip of South America.

Colonies and Empire

Magellan's explorations proved very profitable for Spain. The Philippine Islands became an important Spanish colony when Spanish exploration of the Pacific Ocean resumed in 1570. Large, fast ships known as Spanish galleons made the journey less dangerous and a new route between the two lands was established. Goods were transported from the Philippines to Panama, in Central America, and transported overland and then sent across the Atlantic to Spain. This was a reliable Spanish trading route, and it helped the Philippines become a busy trading post between Spain and the Far East.

(above) The Armada recorded finding seals, sea lions, and other animals on the southern coasts of South America.

Magellan's Memory

Magellan's death in the Philippines had great implications on how he is remembered. His death meant that he could not defend his actions to the Spanish authorities when the Armada returned. The mutineers of the *San Antonio* told a story that protected their own reputations. The *Victoria's* return to Seville did not improve Magellan's reputation. Many of the surviving crew members had taken part in the mutiny. Sebastian Elcano, the *Victoria's* captain and a mutineer, told Spanish officials they mutinied to escape Magellan's brutal rule.

(left) Spice exploration encouraged mapmakers to illustrate their works.

Magellan's Legacy

The travels of Magellan and other explorers influenced the world in many ways. One of the most visible legacies of the Age of Discovery is colonialism. Once new worlds were discovered, countries such as Spain claimed them as their own.

Cultures Lost

Europeans brought new languages, religions, laws, and economies to the territories they colonized. The diseases they carried and had **immunity** to were unknowingly brought to North and South America, where they killed hundreds of thousands of native peoples who had no natural immunity. These deaths meant knowledge of indigenous languages and cultures were lost as there was no one left to tell their stories. The legacy of European travel to North America and South America can still be seen in the languages, religions, and races of the people who live on these continents today.

The Spice Empires

The search for spices brought Europeans, such as Magellan, to new places around the world. Spain and Portugal's race to claim the Spice Islands changed the course of world history. The spice trade became a brutal battleground for European **empires**. Over time, the influence of the Spanish and Portuguese gave way to the English and the Dutch. The natives of the Spice Islands lost control of their lands and were enslaved to feed a growing European desire for cloves, nutmeg, mace, and pepper.

(left) A monument to Magellan in Punta Arenas, Chile. In the Philippines, the native chief who slew Magellan is honored with his own statue.

Fantastic Voyage

Armada diarist Antonio Pigafetta recorded observations about the places he traveled. He created tales of strange lights on the ship's mast that saved the Armada's crew from certain death during storms. He thought these lights were a sign from God that all would be well. Today they are known as St. Elmo's fire, or point discharge, a hot gas that forms around a **conductor**, such as a ship's mast. Pigafetta also wrote about the Teheulche of present-day Argentina and the indigenous peoples of the Philippines. Pigafetta made sense of their customs and languages by asking them questions with hand gestures or body language. Later explorers would try to replicate Magellan's voyage, but it would take almost 60 years before the world was circumnavigated for the second time.

Straits and Clouds

Magellan's name lives on in other ways. The strait he found through South America is now called the Strait of Magellan. A cluster of stars called the Magellanic Clouds were named after him. This formation appears to be a cloud in the night sky, but is actually a faraway **galaxy**. It was discovered as the Armada de Molucca sailed over the Pacific Ocean.

(background) A Magellanic Cloud is a cluster of stars in a far-away galaxy, named after the explorer who headed the first circumnavigation of the world.

Glossary

apprentice Someone who is working and learning a trade or job

Arab A person from the Middle East or North Africa who speaks the Arabic language

cannibal A person who eats the flesh of other humans

cape A point of land that juts out into a body of water

cargo The supplies of the ship

Christianity A religion founded on the life and teachings of Jesus Christ

colonialism When a group of people settle in a distant land but remain citizens of their native country

commend To speak highly of or praise

commission Giving permission to do something or a paid order

commuted To change a punishment or sentence for a crime from more severe to less severe

conductor A substance that provides a path for the flow of electricity, heat, and other energy forms

convert To change one's religion, faith, or beliefs

court A pharaoh or a king and all those around him, including his family, personal servants, advisors, and officials

empires A number of territories or governments controlled by one country

finance To fund, or give money to a cause

galaxy A large group of stars

Holy Roman Empire A group of countries in Europe under the rule of one leader

immunity The ability to resist disease

mass A religious celebration of the Catholic Church

mast A tall pole rising from the deck of a sailing ship that is used to support sails and rigging

mortar A cannon used to fire shells in a high arc

mutiny A rebellion of the ship's crew against its captain

navigator Someone who is trained in methods of determining location

pilot The helmsman of a ship who guides or steers the ship's course

ration A fixed amount or portion, such as food

replenish To add new stock or supplies

riptides A strong, narrow current that flows rapidly away form the shore, returning water carrried toward shore by waves

Roman Catholicism Pertaining to the organization of Christians that is headed by the pope

stocks A wooden device made for punishment with holes for ankles and wrists

strait A narrow waterway connecting two bodies of water

trade winds The winds that blow from the north Atlantic near the equator

Index

1 2 3 4 5 6 7 8 9 0 Printed in the U.S.A. 4 3 2 1 0 9 8 7 6 5